W9-CMO-203

ALWAYS HAVE POPSICLES®

HOW TO BE THE BEST GRANDPARENT
AND REALLY ENJOY YOUR GRANDCHILDREN

BY REBECCA HARVIN

Popsicle® is a registered trademark of Good Humor-Breyers, used with permission.

For inquiries about volume orders, please contact:

Beaufort Books
27 West 20th Street, Suite 1102
New York, NY 10011
sales@beaufortbooks.com

Published in the United States by Beaufort Books
www.beaufortbooks.com

Distributed by Midpoint Trade Books
www.midpointtrade.com

Printed in the United States of America

Interior and Cover design by Avery Designs, Clayton, NC
Cover Illustration by Thomas Badger, Raleigh, NC

DEDICATION

This book is dedicated to all of my grandchildren:

CULLEN
VIRGINIA
MOORE
OSLER
BESSIE ROSE
LUCIUS

Without these wonderful grandchildren, I would not be able to belong to the greatest group—

THE GRANDPARENT GENERATION

*May you live to see your
children's children.*
Psalm 128:6

INTRODUCTION

We see millions of handbooks on how to be the best businessman or woman, best athlete, making it to the top—achieving success in every aspect of life. Well, even if you achieved all your goals, here is the handbook you have been waiting for. This handbook has great advice on how to achieve and experience one of the greatest joys of our life—being a grandparent.

There are so many little things that we can do as a grandparent that will make a big difference.

Because many of our daughters and daughters-in-law are working moms, I believe that being a grandparent is even more important now than ever before.

You will find that some of my suggestions are things that we never had time to do with our own children. We were too busy being a mom, dad, chauffeur, cook, spectator (for sports events, piano and dance recitals, etc.), wife, and husband.

We learn that we cannot do everything at every stage of life. That is why it is so great to have a second chance and be a grand-mom and grand-pop.

Most of the suggestions in this book are for younger children. As my grandchildren grow older, I realize that my role will also change. A teenage grandchild is another ball game or a whole new animal, as some parents see it! Just remember, grandchildren are only small once—enjoy.

Perhaps I shall write another book as my grandchildren grow older and I have an opportunity to experience and enjoy older grandchildren.

Remember your Grandchildren are only
young once

LET THEM BE CHILDREN

When I was a child, I spoke like a child,
I thought like a child, I reasoned like a child;
when I became a man, I gave up childish ways.

1 Corinthians 13:11

Always have an answer to their questions.

Always have a nightlight.

Never close the door all the way.

Always cover them with sunscreen
when outside.

Encourage them to wear a hat in the sun.

Teach them to play Go-Fishing.

Always have peanut butter and jelly.

Tell them about yourself
when you were a little girl or boy.
These stories will be better than fairy tales.

Show them pictures of their parents when they were little.

Let your grandchildren know
at the earliest possible age
that you will not accept behavior
in your home
that is not acceptable to you.

Invite teenage grandchildren
to go on a summer trip with you.
The parents will love you!

Teach them to snap their fingers.

Teach them to do the shag.

Show them toys that their mama and daddy played with.

When your grandchildren are infants
wear the same perfume or aftershave
that their parents wear.

Never make them clean their plate.

Always have dessert.

Encourage them to try new foods.
They will discover something that they love.

Show them how to make real biscuits—
with a rolling pin!

Teach them to knit one, purl two.

Wiggle your ears for them.

Pull a quarter out of their ear.

Teach them to wink.

Watch their favorite television show
with them.
Have them to tell you all about the
characters, etc.

Take older children out to dinner
(not supper).
Require that they dress accordingly.

Teach them the difference between
an appetizer and an entree,
and
tell them why they have so many forks!

Teach them to set a proper table.

Teach them to like bugs.

Keep a magnifying glass
to look at bugs with.

Teach them how to tie a bow ribbon
and a bow tie.

Teach them to flip a coin.

Give them a big box to play with.

Buy them good books—
The Classics, Art Books.

Buy foreign language tapes
and encourage them
to learn and say simple phrases.

Keep a grandchild,
one at a time,
without the parents.

Always have riding toys.

Always have toys with wheels.

Teach them to whistle.

Teach them how to play 1 potato - 2 potato.

Always have their favorite food
when they visit.

Let them pump gas (with your supervision).

Save old things
such as:
telephones, eggbeaters, radios,
kitchen utensils,
rolling pins, etc.
These make great toys.

Take them to a farm.

Take them on a train ride.

Take them to Disney World.

Help them start a picture album.

Help them start a scrapbook.

Have your own grandparent toys.
Make sure you have a girl box and a boy box.

Always prepare for a grandchild's visit
so that you can enjoy their visit to the fullest:

Get extra help.
Cancel all meetings.
Do grocery shopping before they come.
Line up baby sitters if you know you will
need them.

Leave your grandchildren messages
on the answering machine.

Send them an E-mail.

Encourage them to call you
and
tell you what they are up to.

Send mail—

Christmas cards
Birthday cards
Halloween cards
Easter cards
Valentines
Post Cards

Buy them a set of encyclopedias.

Ask them to tell you about their friends.

Take them to the circus.

Take them fishing.
Catch a fish!

Say the blessing at every meal.

Help them say their prayers.

Teach them that
Christmas is a Birthday.

Teach them to write thank-you notes.

Always have Band-Aids.

Always have plastic cups
with snap-on sippy tops.

Give your granddaughter her first manicure.

Ask grandchildren to dance at
family weddings.

Read to them
and
listen to them read a lot.

Expose them to classical music.

Introduce them to your friends.

Encourage them to shake hands and to say
"Nice to meet you!"

Make your house rules clear and consistent.

Play ball games with your grandchildren.

Teach them to watch the ball.
You may contribute to a college education
or early retirement!

Praise them!

Hug them a lot.

Visit your Grandchildren in their home.

Let them show you their room.

Go to their birthday parties.

Go to see them in the Christmas pageant.

Tell your granddaughter she is pretty.

Tell your grandson he is handsome.

Teach them to wrap a pretty present.

ALWAYS HAVE POPSICLES!®

Give them the experience of communicating
with adults.

Take them shopping to buy mom
and dad a present.

Get them their own library card to use when they visit you.

Send granddaughters corsages
for special events.

Let them play in the rain in a bathing suit.

Teach them to walk on stilts.

Read them something before they go to bed
or have them read you something.

Take them to church.

Give them money to put into
the collection plate.

Take them to sports events.

Invite them to visit during
Vacation Bible School.

Introduce your grandchild to a
police officer and firefighter.
Make sure they are in uniform.

Have watermelon parties.

Show them where you went to school.

Make your Grandchildren aware of their heritage.
Tell them all that you know about their families.

Tell your children of it, and let your children tell their children, and their children another generation.
Joel 1:3

Tell them silly jokes.

Laugh together !

Teach them to thread a needle.

Always have flashlights that work,
and teach them how to change the batteries.

Teach them a tune on the piano.

Try to see grandchildren once a month
during the first year.

Catch lightning bugs.
Catch frogs.

Always have empty jars to put them in.

Let them help you cook.

Show them where you work.

Let them use your computer.

Encourage them to read a lot.

Feed the birds.

Make bird food.

Make valentines.

Show them old family photo albums.

Play games with them.
Teach them games you played with
their parents.

Give them little chores at your house.

Start a collection of something that will interest them.

Encourage older children to read the newspaper.

Remind them to always say "please"
and "thank you."

Encourage imagination.

Praise their mother and father.

Emphasize that practice makes perfect.

Take a CPR course.

Cut up meat in itsy bitsy pieces.

Take them to a fire station.

Have a thermometer.

Make cookies with them—
the real kind.
Use a rolling pin.

Always buckle up.

Don't smoke.

Never make them eat anything that they
dislike at your house!

Let them see you eating yucky things,
like okra, stewed tomatoes, and liver.

Take them grocery shopping with you
and let them pick out their favorite cereal.

Put away harmful things,
they will get into as soon as you turn your
back—
pills, detergents, cleaning material, etc.

Let toddlers open your kitchen cabinets
and play with your pots and pans.

Always let them lick the bowl or beaters
when making something good.

Save your old clothes and accessories
for dress up.

Have a "night-night"
when they visit.

One that belonged to their parent is always
special.

Read them their favorite story over and over.

Buy anything that they are selling
to raise money
for their church, school, soccer team, etc.

Occasionally, pop popcorn for them
when they watch their favorite video.

Always keep your promises.

Have a plan and projects for rainy days.

**Keep a craft box handy with:
crayons, tape, glue, scissors.**

Travel with them.

Teach them a neat poem.

Make sure they brush their teeth.

Listen to their prayers.

Tuck them in—
Promise them that the bed bugs won't bite.

Take <u>lots</u> of pictures.

Help them develop nutritious eating habits.

Encourage and help them to save money.

Give them money to blow!

Let them get to know your friends' children
and grandchildren.

They will look forward to seeing these
friends
when they visit you.

Have a jump rope.

Find a roly poly bug
and watch them roll up in a ball and play
dead.

<u>Always</u> have an answer to—WHY?

Teach them to be nice to older people.
Old people love little children.

Take them to a nursing home
to visit a friend or family member.

Tell them about your town.
Show them where their parents
went to school, church, played, etc.

BE PATIENT!

Be calm—
even when they spill grape juice
on your new carpet.

Try to have a grandchildren's room.
Make it fun and full of toys.

Be enthusiastic about things they do and say.

Dig for worms.

Dig holes.

Let them get dirty.

Give them a bath!

Plant a small garden.

Make snow cream.

Make snow balls and put them in the freezer.

Make homemade ice cream.

Start your grandson his first tool box.
Have a:
hammer
nail
screwdriver
saw

Always have balls:

Baseballs
Soccer balls
Basketballs
Tennis balls
Golf balls

Explain why birds migrate and fly in a "V."

Look at the stars.
Find the Big Dipper.

Tell them about the Man in the Moon.

Tell them about George Washington
and the cherry tree.

Teach them the names of flowers.

Watch the sun set with them.

Get up just to watch the sunrise together.

Take them to see the mountains
and the beach.

Walk with them in the rain
with an umbrella.

Teach them to "pump"
so they can swing themselves.

Let them know how special teachers are.

Wear things that sparkle.

Help them to get to know their cousins.

Spoil them !

Send them home when you are tired of them
—or exhausted—
whichever comes first.

Remember, your time, love, and experiences
are the most important things you
can give your grandchildren.

Love them a lot !

Love is patient and kind.

1 Corinthians 13:4

Realize you will not love all of your
grandchildren equally.
You will love each uniquely.

Get to know each child's uniqueness!

Walk on the beach, and look for special shells:

Starfish
Sand Dollars
Baby's Feet

Have an Easter egg dyeing party.

Take them to museums.

Make much ado when your grandchildren
become potty trained and
when they lose their first tooth.

Send your grandchildren pictures of you.

Give them a subscription to a magazine.
Let them pick out what they want.

Take them to a pet store on a rainy day.

Treat your grandchildren's pets
as a member of the family.

Remember, your Grandchildren are children
only once, too

ENJOY THEM !

My grandmother is the greatest just because

She

_____

_____

She

_____

_____

My granddaddy is the greatest just because

He

_____

_____

He

_____

_____